Buffy on the Beach

Sue Steakley

Copyright © 2024
All Rights Reserved

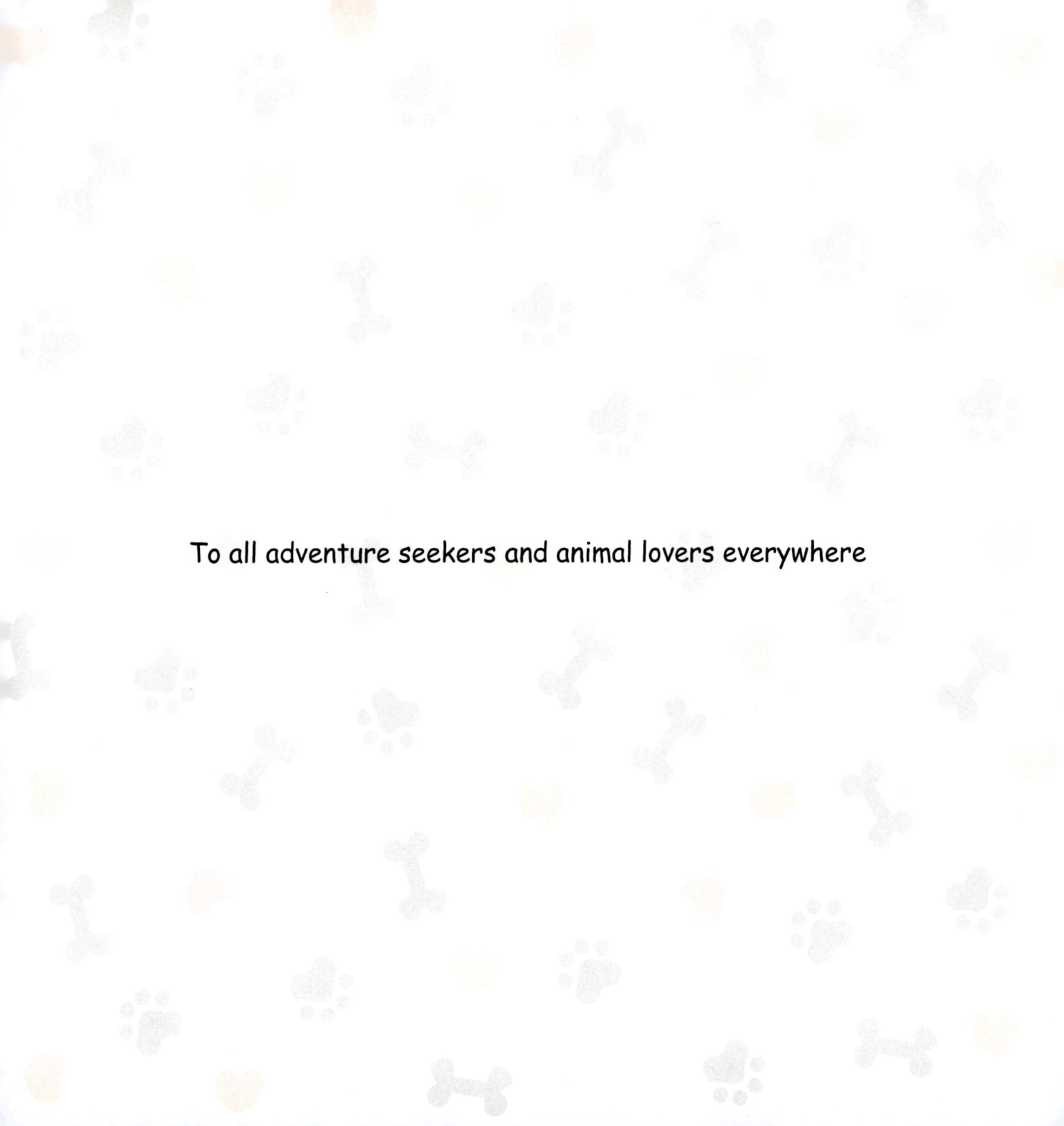

To all adventure seekers and animal lovers everywhere

I dedicate this book to my family and friends, who always encouraged me through the years. And to all animal lovers, who know how very special they are — and to Buffy, whose precious and kind spirit made this possible.

Acknowledgment

I want to dedicate this to my family and friends who have followed along on Buffy's adventures for years and who motivated me to compile this book.

About the Author

The author introduces us to her canine companion, Buffy. Together, they embark on walks along the beach, where Buffy's charming antics become the focal point of a project years in the making. The purpose of the book, aptly titled "Buffy on the Beach", is to convey a simple yet profound message -- small beings can achieve great things! Each photograph is accompanied by thoughtful sayings, creating a synergy of visual and textual storytelling. With meticulous attention to detail, the book paints a vivid picture of the desired aesthetics, emphasizing large, colorful photographs and meaningful sayings. The author's purpose becomes evident - to spread joy, inspiration and a sense of possibility through the charming adventures of Buffy. Join us on this enchanting adventure as Buffy's story comes to life, proving that even in the simplicity of a dog's beachside escapades, there lies a profound lesson for all ages. Get ready to be charmed by Buffy on the Beach, where the tiniest paws leave the biggest paw prints on the sands of inspiration.

Sue, the visionary behind "Buffy on the Beach", brings to life the heartwarming journey of her adorable Maltipoo, Buffy. With a rich background as a professional photographer for 35 years, holding both a Master of Photography Degree and a Camera Craftsman Degree, Sue's love for animals, nature and the ocean shines through her lens. Her passion for capturing the beauty of the world is surpassed only by her dedication to spreading joy and inspiration. Buffy, a small dog with a big heart, became Sue's muse, inspiring a project years in the making. Sue's creative vision, coupled with her meticulous attention to detail, unfolds in the pages of this book. Through charming anecdotes and captivation photographs, she conveys the simple yet profound message that even the smallest beings can achieve greatness. Beyond her artistic pursuits, Sue has a history of contributing to her local community as well as having served on the Advocacy Board of the College of Arts and Sciences at Baylor University. She is an avid world traveller, mother and grandmother enjoying life to the fullest.

Table of Contents

Acknowledgment...4

About the Author...5

Table of Contents..7

Introduction...8

Introduction

"Hi! I'm Buffy! I am excited to take you with me on many of my beach adventures where I have learned so much! I know you will, too! Let's go!"

In the heartwarming and inspiring journey of Buffy, the adorable Maltipoo, a tale unfolds that goes beyond the sandy shores of the Panhandle in Florida. Captured in a delightful collection of photographs, this book tells the story of a small dog with a big heart, proving that even the littlest among us can achieve extraordinary feats.

The author introduces us to her canine companion, Buffy. Together, they embark on walks along the beach where Buffy's charming antics become the focal point of a project years in the making as she builds sandcastles, flies kites and even tries her "paw" at fishing!

"Buffy on the Beach" is not just a book - it is a testament to Sue's belief that every individual, regardless of size, can make a significant impact in this wonderful world.

Live And Be Happy and Make Others Happy Too!

I may be little, but I can do BIG things!

I'm Not Here To Be Average - I'M HERE TO BE AWESOME!!

Many Are Called But Few Go

"Go Big Or Go Home" - It's True! What Have You Got To Lose??

Success Is No Accident - It Is Hard Work, Perseverence, Learning, Studying, Sacrifice And Most Of All, You Must Love What You Are Doing!

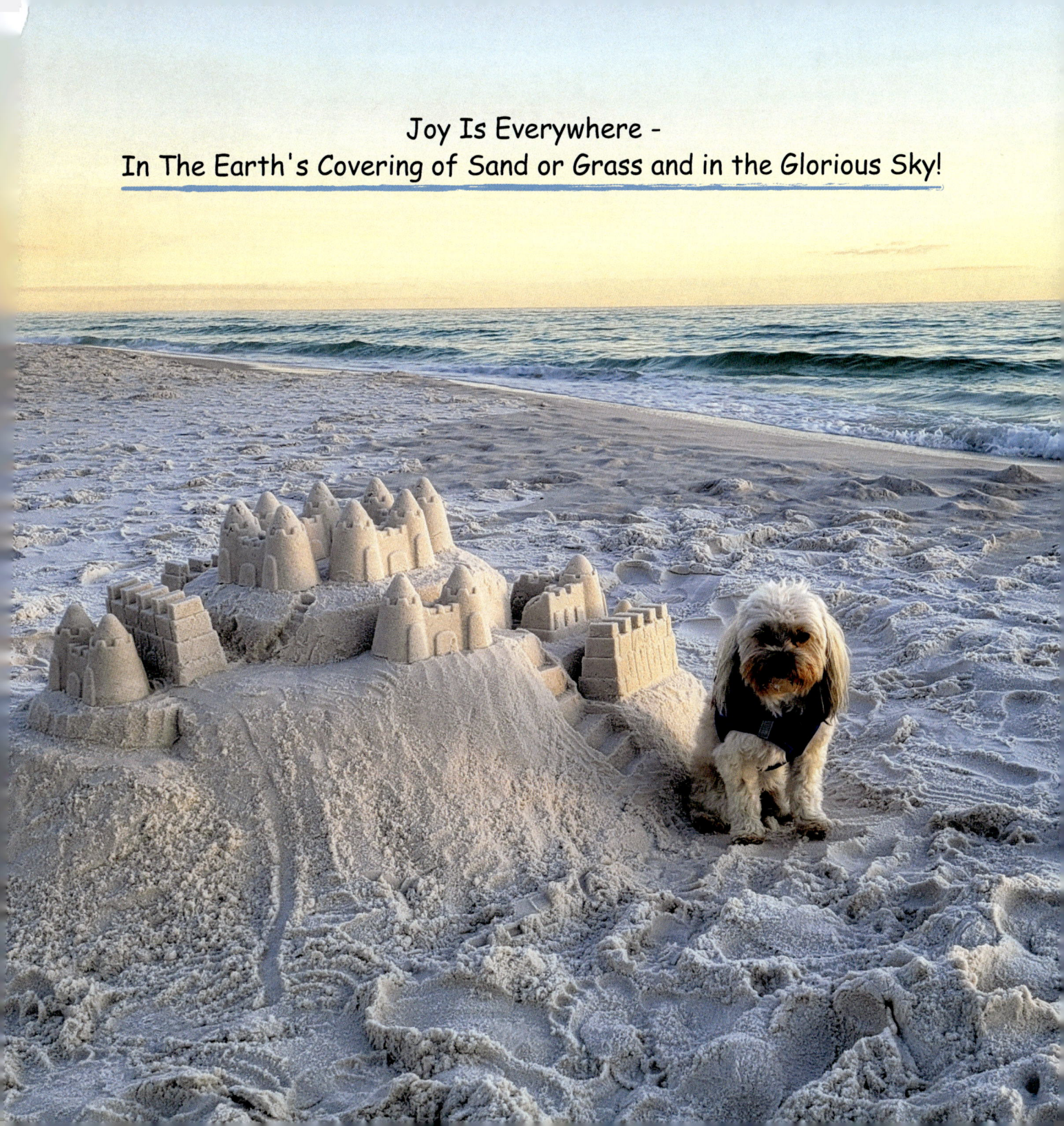

Joy Is Everywhere -
In The Earth's Covering of Sand or Grass and in the Glorious Sky!

There Is Nothing in this Nature World that is not intended to make us happy!

THE GRAYT WALL OF...ART

THE SUPPORT LOCAL ART Y'ALL!

GRAYTON BEACH
NICE DOGS
STRANGE PEOPLE

The most wasted of days is one without laughter!

Start where you are - use what you have - do what you can!

Attitude is a tiny thing that makes a huge difference!

Peace means surrendering illusions of control!

Do one thing every day that scares you!

Happiness lies in the joy of achievement and the thrill of creative effort.

Start with a few and keep going!!!

Make a plan and work it!

No matter how you feel, get up, dress up, show up and NEVER give up!

You can be as big and great as you want to be - just believe in yourself!

Look up! Always!

Start with an idea and let it go!

So many wonders in this world God gave us! Check them out!

Challenges are what makes life interesting.
Overcoming them is what makes life meaningful!

I think
I can!

We all have different gifts and different ways of showing who we are!

Don't build too many walls around yourself!

If you have a unique talent, protect it!

Choose success, not perfection!

Ruins allow you to construct new ideas

Sometimes it's fun to change how we do things!

Aim for the moon! - If you miss, you might hit a star!

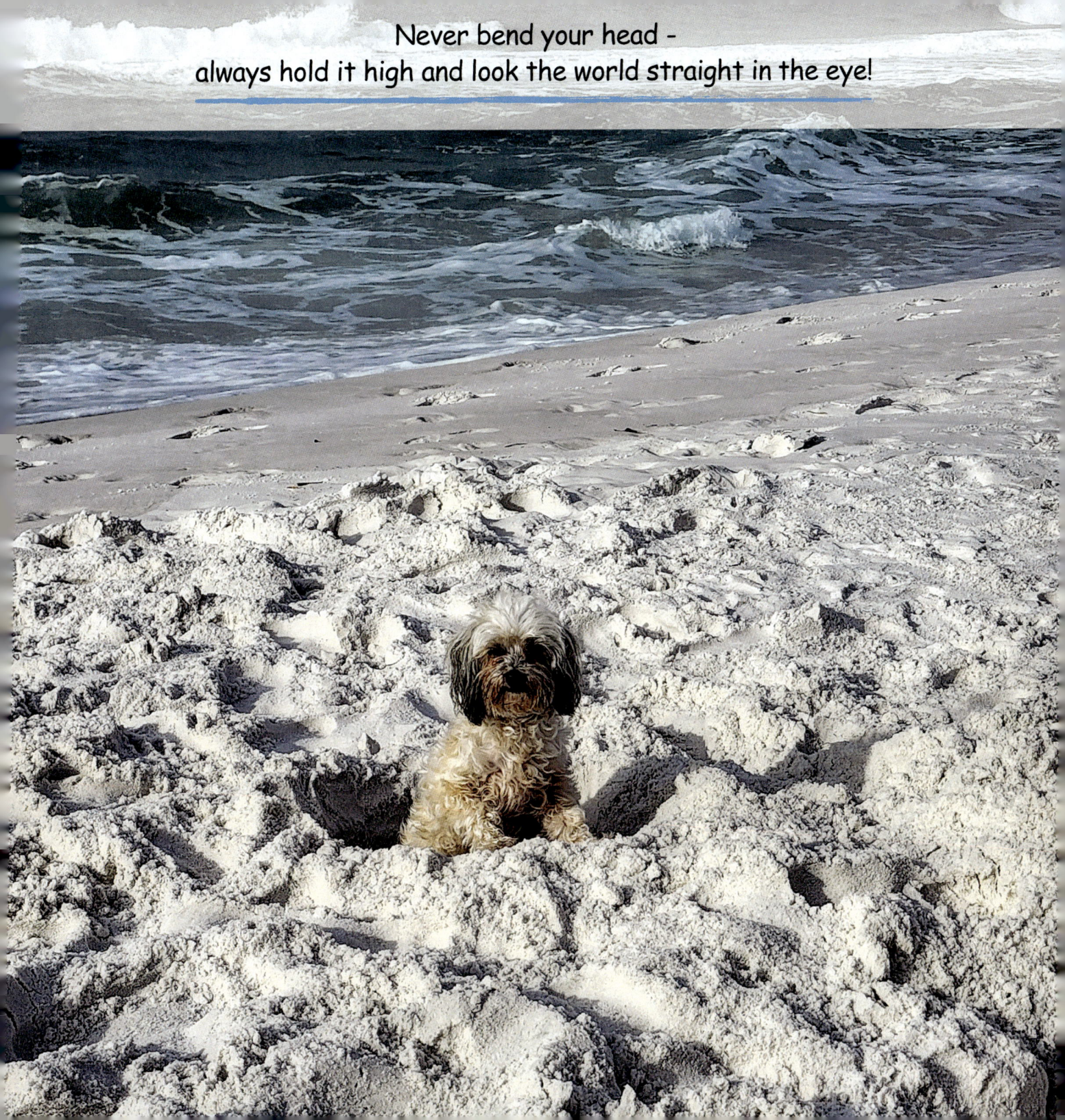

Never bend your head - always hold it high and look the world straight in the eye!

You can't build a reputation on what you're going to do!

Never doubt what you can do, just believe you can do it!

A little rest can invigorate us!

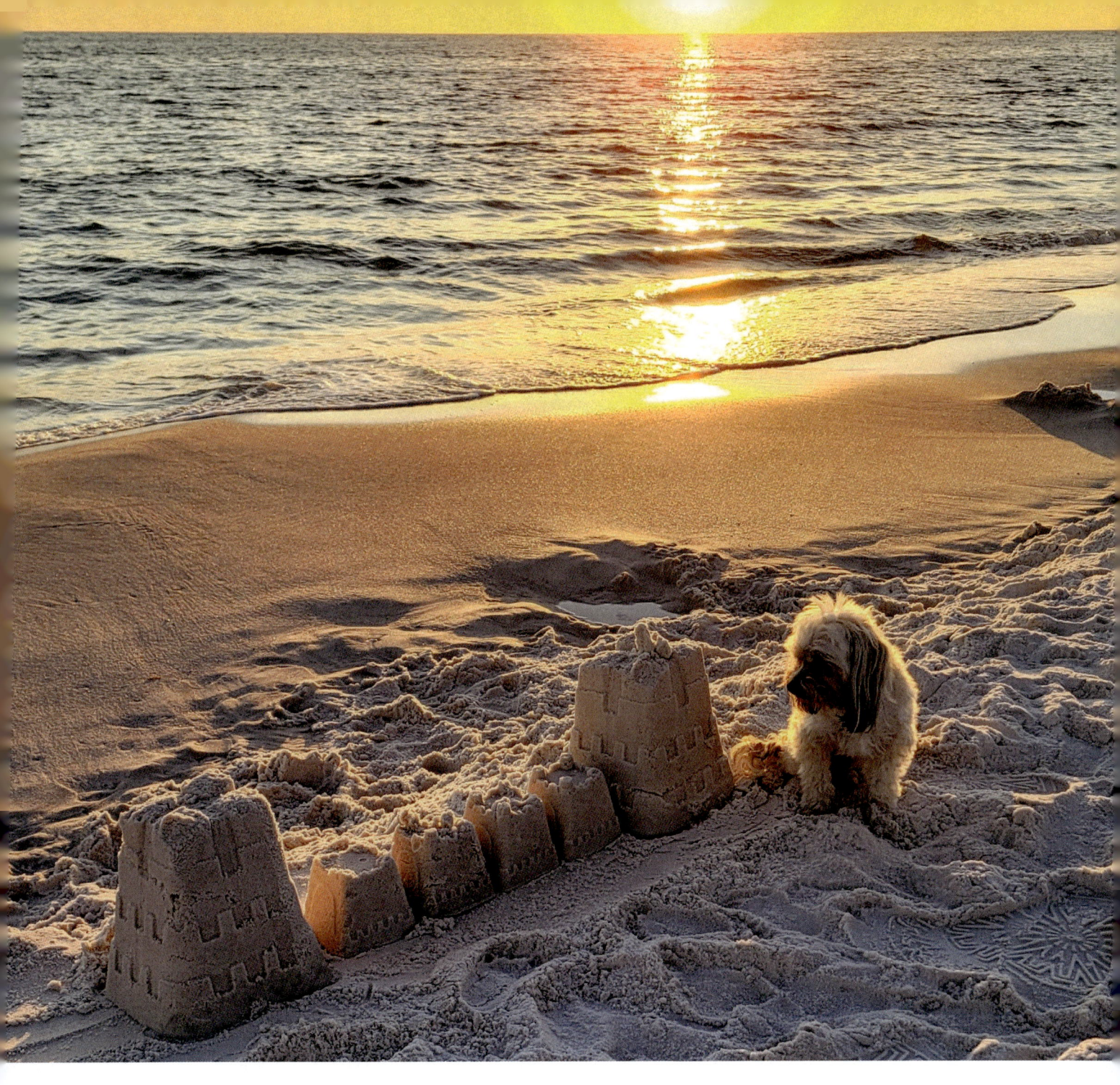

Never put off until tomorrow what you can do today!

If you're lucky enough to find a way of life you love, you just need to find the courage to live it!

We all have abilities - the way we use them is important!

Accept yourself the way you are, but always try to be better!

Don't just dream of success - make it happen!

Imagination is more important than knowledge - knowledge is limited!

Arriving at one's goal is the starting point for another goal!

I am not afraid - I was born to do this!

Believe in your abilities - have faith in yourself!

Take time in your day to enjoy the beauty of this life we have been given!

Feel the wind and what it is saying!

If find beauty in simple things, we will be happy!

Dream big - start small - ACT NOW!

Don't stop when you're tired - stop when you're done!

The meaning of life is in finding your gift - then you will find happiness.

Inspiration comes from inside you -
be POSITIVE and good things will happen!

If you know you can succeed at something, YOU CAN!

Tenderness of heart is a huge benefit of life!

March on and move towards perfection - don't be afraid!

I can, therefore I am!

Nothing is impossible to those who will try!

Happiness is the best, noblest, most pleasant thing in the world!

Deciding to act is sometimes difficult, but the rest is tenacity!

Never get yourself in a hole you can't dig your way out of!

You can talk to your own soul by thinking.

Problems are not stop signs - they are guidelines!

Never quit! Winners never quit and quiters never win!

Where there is a will, there is a way!!!

Your can't find a happy life - you have to MAKE it!

Don't wait for conditions to be perfect to begin -
by beginning, you will make the conditions perfect!

Always be open to discover new things!

The difficult takes time - the impossible takes more.

Touch people with wildlife and they will want to save it!
Peopole save what they love!!

Success isn't always about greatness - it's about consistency; through consistency, success comes which leads to greatness!

Dream it and grab it and never let it go!

Time is never wasted in advance so don't waste a single moment of it!

You must love and feel - it is the reason you are here on Earth!

Dogs do speak but only to those who know how to listen!

Nothing great was ever achieved without much enthusiasm!

If you don't like how things are, change them - you are not a tree!

Always do your best, the benefits are countless!

Do the things you think you cannot do!

No act of kindness, no matter how small, is ever wasted!

All dreams can be achieved - just keep moving towards them!

I am always doing what I cannot do,
in order that I may learn how to do it!

It's not whether you get knocked down, it is whether you get back up!

Success does not mean you don't make mistakes - just don't make them again!

The best motivation for tomorrow is doing your best today!

Even when things get difficult, there are opportunities!!

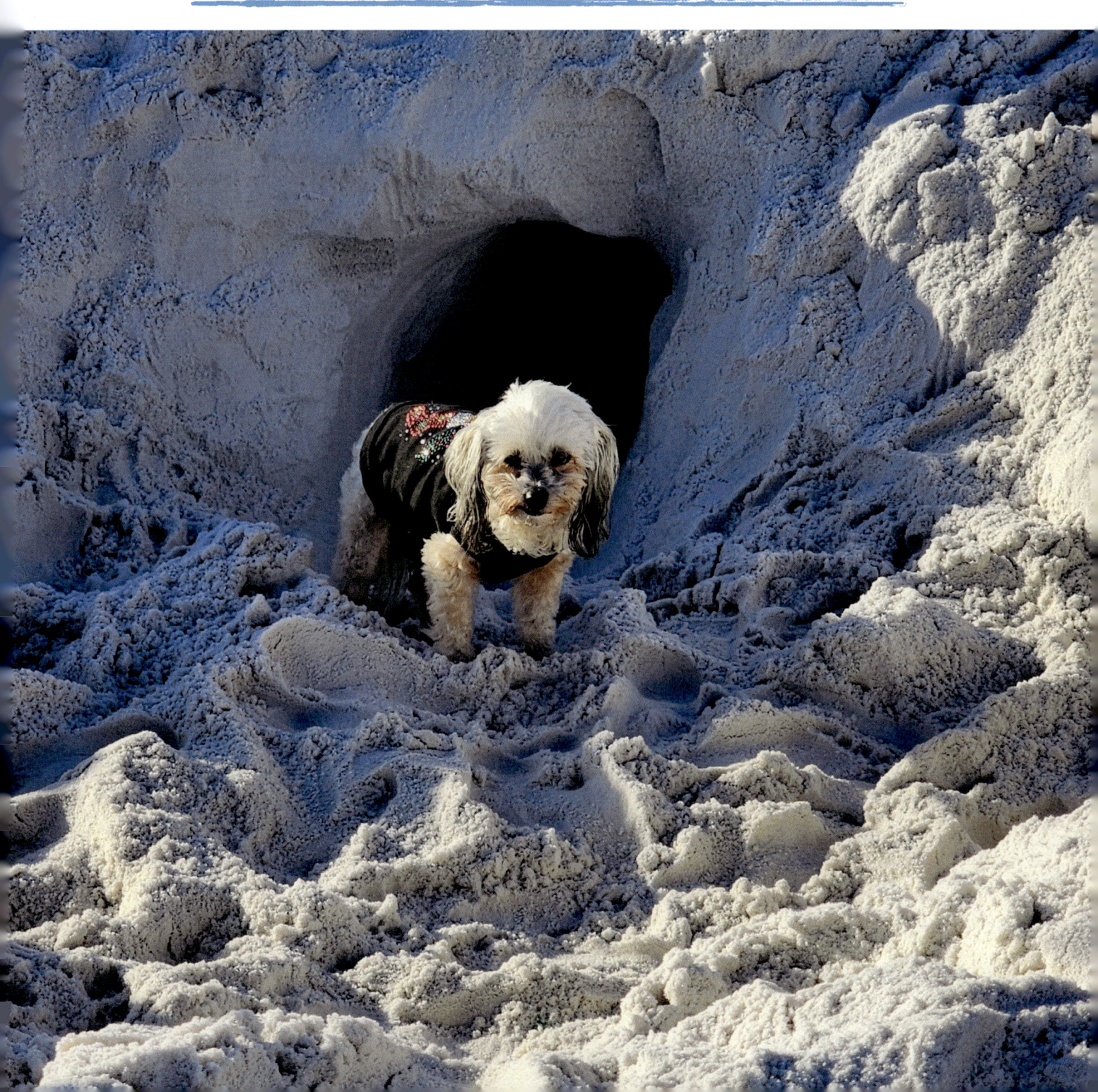

I'd love to see the world in perfect harmony and keep it company!

Don't sit and wait for opportunities to come - get up and make them!

Never retreat - never explain - get it done!

Nothing in life is meant to be feared, only understood!

In a gentle way, you can shake the world!

What is inside us is more important than what is before or beyond us!

The greatest gift you can ever give is your honest self.

Always desire to learn something useful!

There is nothing I cannot do!

Success isn't about how your life looks to others,
it's about how it feels to you!

Sandcastles don't just build themselves, you have to build them!

Happiness is not ready made - it comes from your own actions!

Don't wait for an opportunity to find you, find it first!

Act as if what you do makes a difference, because it does!!

Life is not measured by the breaths we take, but by the moments that take our breath away!!!

It's kind of fun to do the impossible!

I always dreamed of riding a sea turtle and found a way to do it!!

Believe in yourself - even if you don't, pretend you do and soon you will!!

Your mind will take the shape of your thoughts.

Kites rise highest against the wind, not with it!

The power of finding beauty in the
smallest things makes life lovely and happy!

I think, I can,
I think, I can,
I know, I can!

Be curious, but be cautious

If you can't build a snowman, build a sandman!

Don't hide your talent! A sun-dial is no good in the shade!

Try not to be too serious all the time!
And if you don't already have a dog, get one!

See you at the beach!